Dear Parent:
Your child's love of reading starts here!

Every child learns to read in a different way and at his or her own speed. Some go back and forth between reading levels and read favorite books again and again. Others read through each level in order. You can help your young reader improve and become more confident by encouraging his or her own interests and abilities. From books your child reads with you to the first books he or she reads alone, there are I Can Read Books for every stage of reading:

SHARED READING
Basic language, word repetition, and whimsical illustrations, ideal for sharing with your emergent reader

BEGINNING READING
Short sentences, familiar words, and simple concepts for children eager to read on their own

READING WITH HELP
Engaging stories, longer sentences, and language play for developing readers

READING ALONE
Complex plots, challenging vocabulary, and high-interest topics for the independent reader

ADVANCED READING
Short paragraphs, chapters, and exciting themes for the perfect bridge to chapter books

I Can Read Books have introduced children to the joy of reading since 1957. Featuring award-winning authors and illustrators and a fabulous cast of beloved characters, I Can Read Books set the standard for beginning readers.

A lifetime of discovery begins with the magical words **"I Can Read!"**

Visit www.icanread.com for information
on enriching your child's reading experience.

For Elkie and the friends
you make along the way
—R.S.

I Can Read Book® is a trademark of HarperCollins Publishers.

Splat the Cat: Splat and Seymour, Best Friends Forevermore
Copyright © 2014 by Rob Scotton
All rights reserved. Manufactured in China.
No part of this book may be used or reproduced in any manner whatsoever without written permission except in the case of brief quotations
embodied in critical articles and reviews. For information address HarperCollins Children's Books, a division of HarperCollins Publishers, 195
Broadway, New York, NY 10007.
www.icanread.com

Library of Congress catalog card number: 2014933029
ISBN 978-0-06-211603-1 (trade bdg.) —ISBN 978-0-06-211601-7 (pbk.)

14 15 16 17 18 SCP 10 9 8 7 6 5 4 3 2 1 ❖ First Edition

I Can Read!™

BEGINNING
1
READING

Splat the Cat

Splat and Seymour,
Best Friends Forevermore

Based on the bestselling books by Rob Scotton

Cover art by Rick Farley

Text by Alissa Heyman

Interior illustrations by Robert Eberz

HARPER

An Imprint of HarperCollinsPublishers

Splat and Seymour were best friends.

They did everything together.

"You and me," said Splat.

"Me and you," Seymour said.

"Friends forevermore!"

"What can I do

for my favorite friend,

the friend I adore?" wondered Splat.

"I know. I'll throw Seymour

the best surprise party ever,

with treats and games galore!"

"Let's see!
There has to be
cake and ice cream and candy,
horns and streamers and balloons,
fancy hats and much, much more!"

The next morning, when Splat ran

to call all his friends,

Seymour ran, too.

Uh-oh, Splat thought.

How can I plan or go to the store

when I'm always with my friend Seymour?

Splat tiptoed into the kitchen
to whisper his plan to his mom.
"That's great," she said.
"But how can you get out the door
without Seymour?"
"I have an idea!" said Splat.

"Seymour, why don't you

play with Little Sis?" said Splat.

"Mom and I have to go to the store,

and it's going to be such a bore."

Seymour nodded, but he was surprised.

He'd never been left at home before.

At the store, Splat piled the cart
with more and more. . . .
There were too many
yummy ice cream flavors
for him to ignore!

At home, Splat told Seymour,

"I have to do some chores.

Plank said you can visit him,

and you two can play outdoors.

Won't that be fun?"

Seymour nodded, but he was puzzled.

Why would Splat

want him to play with Plank?

Splat and Seymour

had always done everything

together before.

Splat went to work.

He baked a cheese cake

for Seymour's party.

Then he baked four more.

He cooked cheese swirl cookies,

but Splat still wanted more.

He made a huge bowl

of chocolate cheese pudding.

"Spike is playing a soccer game,
and he asked me to keep score.
I'll be back before you can shout."
Seymour's whiskers drooped.
Why was Splat leaving him out?

Splat pedaled fast.

He invited all his classmates.

Then he invited more:

even Mrs. Wimpydimple

and the cat twins next door.

Finally, it was party day.

Splat had to get Seymour away.

"Seymour, I promised Kitten

I would play with her,

but I have to do more chores.

Could you go over without me?"

Seymour liked Kitten, so he agreed.

But he felt sad.

Didn't Splat want him

around anymore?

Splat had to decorate fast.

He hung bright streamers.

He blew up colorful balloons.

And then he blew up more.

And more.

If only Seymour knew
what was in store!
Splat had even made
a banner that read,

IT'S SEYMOUR'S PARTY DAY!

Kitten was decorating, too.

She was decorating Seymour.

"Let's play dress-up.

Look, here's a fancy outfit

that my doll once wore."

Kitten held out a mirror,

and Seymour jumped in surprise.

"As great as this outfit is,

it's not my style," he said.

"I'm sorry that was such a bore.

I found just the thing," said Kitten.

It's a fairy dress and sparkling wand!

You can be a fairy princess to adore."

"No more, no more!"

yelled Seymour.

"Splat, I'm coming home,

even if you don't love me anymore."

Seymour came in the door.

His tail and whiskers sagged.

He had never felt so alone before.

"Surprise!" everybody yelled.

Splat yelled the loudest.

Seymour's eyes opened wide

at the uproar.

"A party? A party just for me?

That's why you kept me away!

Hooray!"

Seymour ate ice cream and cake,

and candy and popcorn,

and cheese galore.

He opened presents.

He ate some more.

But best of all, he was with Splat again!

"Oh, Splat," squeaked Seymour.

"This was the best party ever!"

"You and me," said Splat.

"Me and you," Seymour said.

"Friends forevermore!"